WELCOME...

This journal is to be used in accompaniment with therapy. Its goal is to aid you in purposeful reflection about your therapy journey. You can use this journal to write down any reflections from your sessions, your concerns, or to take notes about topics you would like to discuss.

Writing your thoughts can help with processing your thoughts and feelings and can bring significant insight about your therapy experience.

There are some hefty benefits to journaling. Therapists often recommend keeping a journal because of the potential benefits.

These benefits include:
-documenting your feelings in the moment to reduce the intensity of the emotion
-using the journal as a reflection tool to help you gain insight
-helps process and make sense of things
-keeping track of goals and the plans you take to follow through
-documenting affirmations, mantras, scriptures, inspiring quotes

This journal would also be helpful if you have a session and experience "therapy hangover" afterwards. "Therapy hangover" can happen following a session that may have been particularly exhausting. You may feel tired, overwhelmed, triggered, or want to cope in an unhealthy way. This journal will prompt you to identify ways you can engage in self-care post-session.

Each session will have an outline to explore the full therapy experience before, during, and after the session.

Before session: document any thoughts, concerns, or topics you'd like to cover in session.

During session: to document any helpful insights or tools explored in the session

After session: this is to review any thoughts, actions, or feelings as a result of the session.

There will also be extra pages so you can free write any other thoughts or reflections from the sessions and beyond. This journal will be a helpful tool for reflecting on your experience with therapy.

I want to thank you for choosing this journal. I hope it serves you well. Remember, your healing experience is unique to you. This is YOUR journey.

I decided to call this journal "Simply Being" because to simply be is to accept and honor yourself as you are right now. This includes how you care for yourself as you navigate life's experiences, the difficult and the joyous.

The pages of this journal should cover three to four months of weekly sessions.

May this journal be a helpful guide, support, and bring you much insight.

-Krystal C. Jackson

Therapist LPC

JOURNAL PROMPTS

What does my ideal life look like?

What am I releasing today?

What emotions do I feel the most today?

On a scale of 1-10, how strongly do I feel
___________ emotion?

Identify three ways I can engage in self-care
today

What am I most concerned about today?

What am I most grateful for today?

Who do I need for support today?

Identify a few things that bring you joy?

JOURNAL PROMPTS

Favorite quote, mantra, or affirmation

Write about the last time you conquered a fear?

Identify a few ways you can self-soothe.

What are my current life priorities?

Name something you want to do but have been afraid to do.

FEELINGS LIST

Adventurous	Free	Proud
Amazed	Frustrated	Radiant
Angry	Furious	Rejuvenated
Annoyed	Grieving	Relieved
Anxious	Grounded	Resentful
Appreciative	Happy	Sad
Ashamed	Hopeful	Satisfied
Bitter	Hurt	Scared
Bliss	Inadequate	Self-conscious
Bored	Indifferent	Shocked
Brave	Insecure	Silly
Comfortable	Inspired	Stupid
Confused	Interested	
Content	Irritated	Suspicious
		Tense
Depressed	Jealous	Terrified
Determined	Joy	Thankful
Disdain	Lonely	Trapped
Disgusted	Lost	Uncomfortable
Eager	Loving	
		Vibrant
Embarrassed	Miserable	Warm
Energetic	Motivated	Weary
Envious	Nervous	Worn Out
Excited	Overwhelmed	Worried
Exhausted	Passionate	Worthy
Foolish	Peaceful	
	Playful	

BEFORE SESSION

How do I feel today?
What emotions are most prominent?
What topics do I want to discuss today?Identify any thoughts
(helpful or unhelpful) that are on your mind today?

SESSION #:

DATE

DURING SESSION

What resources were given?
Homework?
Any "aha" moments?

AFTER SESSION

How are you feeling?
What emotion(s) are you experiencing?
Level of intensity of the emotion 1-10
Identify a self-care activity to engage in
Who can support me today?

REFLECTIONS

REFLECTIONS

REFLECTIONS

BEFORE SESSION

How do I feel today?
What emotions are most prominent?
What topics do I want to discuss today?Identify any thoughts
(helpful or unhelpful) that are on your mind today?

DURING SESSION

What resources were given?
Homework?
Any "aha" moments?

SESSION #: _______________________________

DATE _______________________________

AFTER SESSION

How are you feeling?
What emotion(s) are you experiencing?
Level of intensity of the emotion 1-10
Identify a self-care activity to engage in
Who can support me today?

REFLECTIONS

REFLECTIONS

REFLECTIONS

BEFORE SESSION

How do I feel today?
What emotions are most prominent?
What topics do I want to discuss today?Identify any thoughts
(helpful or unhelpful) that are on your mind today?

DURING SESSION

What resources were given?
Homework?
Any "aha" moments?

AFTER SESSION

How are you feeling?
What emotion(s) are you experiencing?
Level of intensity of the emotion 1-10
Identify a self-care activity to engage in
Who can support me today?

REFLECTIONS

REFLECTIONS

REFLECTIONS

BEFORE SESSION

How do I feel today?
What emotions are most prominent?
What topics do I want to discuss today?Identify any thoughts
(helpful or unhelpful) that are on your mind today?

DURING SESSION

What resources were given?
Homework?
Any "aha" moments?

AFTER SESSION

How are you feeling?
What emotion(s) are you experiencing?
Level of intensity of the emotion 1-10
Identify a self-care activity to engage in
Who can support me today?

REFLECTIONS

REFLECTIONS

REFLECTIONS

"

My past doesn't define my future. Everyday is a fresh start with a new beginning to make my own.

____

BEFORE SESSION

How do I feel today?
What emotions are most prominent?
What topics do I want to discuss today?Identify any thoughts
(helpful or unhelpful) that are on your mind today?

DURING SESSION

What resources were given?
Homework?
Any "aha" moments?

AFTER SESSION

How are you feeling?
What emotion(s) are you experiencing?
Level of intensity of the emotion 1-10
Identify a self-care activity to engage in
Who can support me today?

REFLECTIONS

REFLECTIONS

REFLECTIONS

BEFORE SESSION

How do I feel today?
What emotions are most prominent?
What topics do I want to discuss today?Identify any thoughts
(helpful or unhelpful) that are on your mind today?

DURING SESSION

What resources were given?
Homework?
Any "aha" moments?

AFTER SESSION

How are you feeling?
What emotion(s) are you experiencing?
Level of intensity of the emotion 1-10
Identify a self-care activity to engage in
Who can support me today?

REFLECTIONS

REFLECTIONS

REFLECTIONS

SESSION #: ______________________

DATE: ______________________

BEFORE SESSION

How do I feel today?
What emotions are most prominent?
What topics do I want to discuss today?Identify any thoughts
(helpful or unhelpful) that are on your mind today?

____

____

____

____

____

____

____

____

____

____

____

____

____

____

DURING SESSION

What resources were given?
Homework?
Any "aha" moments?

AFTER SESSION

How are you feeling?
What emotion(s) are you experiencing?
Level of intensity of the emotion 1-10
Identify a self-care activity to engage in
Who can support me today?

REFLECTIONS

REFLECTIONS

REFLECTIONS

SESSION #:

DATE:

BEFORE SESSION

How do I feel today?
What emotions are most prominent?
What topics do I want to discuss today?Identify any thoughts
(helpful or unhelpful) that are on your mind today?

DURING SESSION

What resources were given?
Homework?
Any "aha" moments?

AFTER SESSION

How are you feeling?
What emotion(s) are you experiencing?
Level of intensity of the emotion 1-10
Identify a self-care activity to engage in
Who can support me today?

REFLECTIONS

REFLECTIONS

REFLECTIONS

66

Healing is an art. It takes time, it takes practice. It takes love.

BEFORE SESSION

How do I feel today?
What emotions are most prominent?
What topics do I want to discuss today?Identify any thoughts
(helpful or unhelpful) that are on your mind today?

SESSION #: ________________________

DATE ________________________

DURING SESSION

What resources were given?
Homework?
Any "aha" moments?

____

____

____

____

____

____

____

____

____

____

____

____

____

____

AFTER SESSION

How are you feeling?
What emotion(s) are you experiencing?
Level of intensity of the emotion 1-10
Identify a self-care activity to engage in
Who can support me today?

REFLECTIONS

REFLECTIONS

REFLECTIONS

REFLECTIONS

BEFORE SESSION

How do I feel today?
What emotions are most prominent?
What topics do I want to discuss today?Identify any thoughts
(helpful or unhelpful) that are on your mind today?

____

____

____

____

____

____

____

____

____

____

____

____

____

____

DURING SESSION

What resources were given?
Homework?
Any "aha" moments?

AFTER SESSION

How are you feeling?
What emotion(s) are you experiencing?
Level of intensity of the emotion 1-10
Identify a self-care activity to engage in
Who can support me today?

REFLECTIONS

REFLECTIONS

REFLECTIONS

SESSION #:

DATE:

BEFORE SESSION

How do I feel today?
What emotions are most prominent?
What topics do I want to discuss today?Identify any thoughts
(helpful or unhelpful) that are on your mind today?

DURING SESSION

What resources were given?
Homework?
Any "aha" moments?

AFTER SESSION

How are you feeling?
What emotion(s) are you experiencing?
Level of intensity of the emotion 1-10
Identify a self-care activity to engage in
Who can support me today?

REFLECTIONS

REFLECTIONS

REFLECTIONS

BEFORE SESSION

How do I feel today?
What emotions are most prominent?
What topics do I want to discuss today?Identify any thoughts
(helpful or unhelpful) that are on your mind today?

DURING SESSION

What resources were given?
Homework?
Any "aha" moments?

AFTER SESSION

How are you feeling?
What emotion(s) are you experiencing?
Level of intensity of the emotion 1-10
Identify a self-care activity to engage in
Who can support me today?

REFLECTIONS

REFLECTIONS

REFLECTIONS

66

Words have power.
You are what you say to yourself.

____

DATE:

BEFORE SESSION

How do I feel today?
What emotions are most prominent?
What topics do I want to discuss today?Identify any thoughts
(helpful or unhelpful) that are on your mind today?

SESSION #: _______________________

DATE _______________________

DURING SESSION

What resources were given?
Homework?
Any "aha" moments?

____

____

____

____

____

____

____

____

____

____

____

____

____

____

AFTER SESSION

How are you feeling?
What emotion(s) are you experiencing?
Level of intensity of the emotion 1-10
Identify a self-care activity to engage in
Who can support me today?

REFLECTIONS

REFLECTIONS

REFLECTIONS

BEFORE SESSION

How do I feel today?
What emotions are most prominent?
What topics do I want to discuss today?Identify any thoughts
(helpful or unhelpful) that are on your mind today?

SESSION #:

DATE

DURING SESSION

What resources were given?
Homework?
Any "aha" moments?

AFTER SESSION

How are you feeling?
What emotion(s) are you experiencing?
Level of intensity of the emotion 1-10
Identify a self-care activity to engage in
Who can support me today?

REFLECTIONS

REFLECTIONS

REFLECTIONS

REFLECTIONS

REFLECTIONS

66

Everyday in every way I am getting healthier and healthier.

———————————

CONGRATULATIONS!!

You've reached the end of this journal.

I hope you gained many insights and look back over the weeks to see your progress. You are doing great and have accomplished so much! Remember, healing is not a linear process, healing happens over time. Keep getting to know yourself and learn to simply be!

This book is a product from Krystal Jackson, a Licensed Professional Counselor. She is the Owner of Simply Being Wellness Counseling in CT. She also hosts a podcast called, "Evolving With Krystal J." which encourages women to embrace the healing journey and accept who they are as they are evolving.

For more information, visit krystalcjackson.com

9 781678 130077